Philip Ardagh's Shortcuts

A FAST
AND FUNNY
GUIDE TO

Florence
Nightingale

Philip Ardagh's Shortcuts

Elizabeth I
Florence Nightingale
Henry VIII
Julius Caesar
Marie Curie
Mary, Queen of Scots
Napoleon
Oliver Cromwell
Queen Victoria
William the Conqueror

Philip Ardagh's Shortcuts

A FAST AND FUNNY GUIDE TO

Florence Nightingale

Illustrated by Alan Rowe

MACMILLAN CHILDREN'S BOOKS

For the staff of Lewisham Hospital,
with memories of a ruptured appendix

First published 1999 by Macmillan Children's Books

This edition published 2013 by Macmillan Children's Books
a division of Macmillan Publishers Limited
20 New Wharf Road, London N1 9RR
Basingstoke and Oxford
Associated companies throughout the world
www.panmacmillan.com

ISBN 978-1-4472-4028-0

1 3 5 7 9 8 6 4 2

A CIP catalogue record for this book is available from the British Library.

Printed and bound by CPI Group (UK) Ltd, Croydon CR0 4YY

CONTENTS

SEBASTOPOL

CRIME[A]

BLACK

CONSTANTINOPLE

SCUTARI

TURKEY

USEFUL WORDS
(Some more useful than others)

Aristocrat At the very least, a lord or lady. A member of the aristocracy or nobility. One of the upper 'upper classes'.

Grand Tour A leisurely trip through the major cities of Europe. It could last for years!

Harley Street A street in London still famous for its (private) doctors' surgeries and clinics.

Hygiene The science of keeping healthy through keeping things – and that includes yourself – nice and clean.

Medicine The medical profession. (In other words, 'studying medicine' doesn't simply mean staring at the yucky-tasting stuff in bottles.)

Orderlies In army hospitals, these were soldiers helping out as attendants. Often drunk and *dis*orderly.

Philanthropist Someone who cares about other people, giving time and money – sometimes *lots* of money – to help them.

Profession A job for which you need special study or training.

Sewer Where sewage goes once it's been flushed or poured down the drain. Where it goes after the sewer, I dread to think. Florence's hospital was built on a blocked sewer.

LITTLE FLO – THE EARLY YEARS

Florence Nightingale was named after the city of Florence, where she was born on 12 May 1820. Before Florence (the person) became famous, there were very few girls called 'Florence' around. Her parents, William and Fanny Nightingale, were English and Florence was their second child. She had a big sister called Parthenope, born in the city of Naples the year before. The original Parthenope was a character in Greek mythology whose drowned body was tossed ashore onto the very spot where Naples was later built. The Nightingales obviously had a thing about cities!

MEET THE FOLKS

Florence's father, William Nightingale, was actually born William Shore. He took the name 'Nightingale' as part of the agreement to inherit money and property from an uncle. If he hadn't, it might have been Florence Shore who was the famous 'Lady with the Lamp'. Florence's mother, Fanny, was considered a great beauty. She had been planning to marry an aristocrat but, when she discovered that he didn't have much money, she married the wealthy William instead!

AN IDYLLIC CHILDHOOD

Not long after Florence's birth, the Nightingales returned to England and to their family home, Lea Hall, in the village of Lea in Derbyshire. The Nightingales were rich, and Lea Hall was a great big rambling house with huge gardens. It was here that little Florence spent her early years. She had a privileged upbringing with everything money could buy . . . but there were clues in her childhood as to what her future would bring.

DOLLS' HOSPITAL

Florence loved looking after her 'sick' dolls. Often, she would decide that one was ill and that it must be allowed to rest without being disturbed. Other times she would announce that one of her — or her sister's — dolls was injured, and would wrap its head or limb in bandages. Many dolls in those days had faces made of wax or china, so really could be injured very easily!

IT'S A DOG'S LIFE

The story goes that Florence's first real live patient was an injured dog called Cap, and that she saved its life. When Florence was ten, she learnt that Cap had a broken leg and was to be put to sleep. She insisted that she could nurse it back to health, and pleaded that the dog's life be spared, which it was. True to her word, she nursed Cap and it lived to chase plenty more sticks and to bury plenty more bones . . . actually it was a sheep dog.

HOME FROM HOME

As well as Lea Hall in Derbyshire, the Nightingales had a country home in Hampshire called Embley Park. Later, they moved out of Lea Hall and into a new home called Lea

Hurst, which William Nightingale had built especially for the family. They spent July to October in Lea Hurst, and the rest of the year at Embley Park – except for March. That was when the Nightingales usually stayed in Mayfair in London, at the Burlington Hotel, for the 'Season'. The Season was the highlight of the 'Society' calendar. The family also spent a great deal of time abroad, with their own six-horse stagecoach and band of servants.

HIGH SOCIETY

A woman of such high social standing as Florence (i.e. rich and posh) was expected to spend her time in Society. Society in this case – not to be confused with ordinary society – meant the privileged class of people (thought to be fashionable) and also referred to the events that made up their social calendar. A well-to-do woman would attend parties, dances and balls and not do a stroke of work (except, perhaps, to tell the servants what to do). When she was old enough, she would be expected to marry into an equally rich (or even richer) and respectable family.

Is this why they call it HIGH society?

YOUNG LADIES OF BREEDING

Like all fine young ladies of the day, Florence and Parthenope learnt reading, music and embroidery but – unusually – their father also insisted that he give them private tuition on other subjects. Florence loved her father's more thought-provoking lessons. Parthenope did not. Florence soon became good at Latin, Greek, French, German, Italian, History and Philosophy.

A THIRST FOR LEARNING

Having been taught far more than a young gentlewoman might expect to learn, Florence wanted more. She wanted to learn maths . . . something which even surprised her father! He was against the idea to begin with, because brainy and knowledgeable women weren't particularly well thought of. Who wanted a wife who might have her own opinions and know more than her husband? This was dangerous stuff! (Don't blame me. I'm just telling you the views of the day.) Finally, Mr Nightingale agreed, and he found Florence a maths tutor.

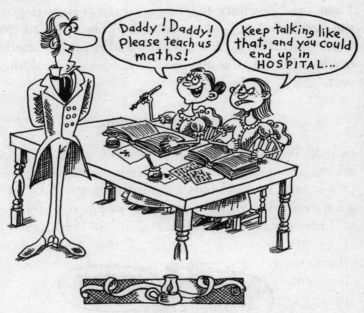

A RELIGIOUS DIVIDE

The Nightingales were Christians but didn't follow the main branch of Christianity in England, the Church of England. They were Unitarians. The big difference between the two was that the Church of England stated that God, Jesus and the Holy Ghost were all one and the same (making up the 'Holy Trinity'), while the Unitarians said that they were not. In other words, Jesus was the son of God, but not actually God.

Later, while Florence and her father remained Unitarians, her mother and Parthenope joined the Church of England. Loyalties within the Nightingale family often split this way too.

OTHER IDEAS

Florence had decided, long ago, that there was much more to life than dances and parties and marrying the right man. Then, on 7 February 1837, when she was sixteen years old, she believed that God spoke to her. She believed that she was being called to do good work and to make something of her life. But what could she do? God hadn't told her that part.

BACK TO EUROPE

In 1838, not long after this revelation – which Florence told no one about at the time – the Nightingale family went off on a tour of Europe. This was no ordinary holiday, not even a long one. The trip lasted almost *two* years! Grand Tours of Europe were very popular amongst the English upper

classes. If you didn't need to work to earn money, you could go abroad and enjoy the paintings and buildings of other cultures.

PEN TO PAPER

These travels abroad didn't just open Florence's eyes to the delights of fine art and architecture. She also witnessed terrible poverty just a stone's throw from the grandness and opulence the tour provided, and she made a point of recording what she saw in her diaries.

PLANS ON HOLD

All that time away from home meant that Florence had to put any plans she might have on hold. By the time they returned to England, she was utterly convinced that she must help the sick, hungry and poor, but still wasn't sure *how*. She started very simply; by taking old clothes, food and medicine to the poor and sick in her neighbourhood. But she wanted to do more. Much more.

PRESENTED TO THE QUEEN

In 1839, Florence, her sister Parthenope and two of their cousins were 'presented' at Queen Victoria's birthday party. This was a way of officially introducing 'young ladies' into grown-up society . . . posh society, remember.

THE FAMOUS LORD PALMERSTON

The Nightingales' neighbour at Embley Park, their winter home, was someone by the name of Palmerston. He lived a couple of miles away in a house called Broadlands. When Florence and her family first moved to Embley Park, in 1825, Palmerston was an up-and-coming young politician. By the time Florence was ten, he'd become Secretary of State for Foreign Affairs, which was a very important job in government. In later years, during the Crimean War – the period in history which made Florence Nightingale most famous – he'd got the top job of Prime Minister.

FRIENDS IN HIGH PLACES

Palmerston often visited Embley Park and the Nightingales often visited Broadlands. It's said that he enjoyed Florence's quick wit and knowledge, but probably wasn't so thrilled by her appalling piano playing. She was well known for being

really bad at it! In later life, Florence would find her friendship with such an important person very useful.

A TRIP TO THE WARDS

Embley Park was near Salisbury, where there was a hospital. Like all hospitals in those days, it was overcrowded with patients, very dirty, very smelly and very noisy. In 1844, aged 24, Florence announced that she wanted to learn to be a nurse there. Her parents were shocked enough that their daughter should want to get any kind of job . . . but a *nurse*? That was unheard of. 'It was as if I had wanted to be a kitchen maid,' Florence later wrote. Her parents forbade it, which is a posh way of saying 'N–O'.

NOT A PROFESSION

Throughout most of the 19th century, hospitals, surgery and nursing were a real hit-and-miss affair. Nursing wasn't a profession. It was a job usually carried out by uneducated women, who couldn't find work elsewhere and were often drunk. This was in the days before people even knew that there were such things as germs or that dirt could carry disease. It's hard to believe now, but that's how it was then. For many patients, a hospital was a place you went into as a last resort, and came out of in a coffin.

MRS GAMP

Charles Dickens, the famous author living and writing at the time, wrote a book called Martin Chuzzlewit which included a character

called Mrs Gamp. This dreadful old woman, with disgusting habits, horrible grimy clothes and a fondness for drinking gin, was a midwife and nurse! Far from being accused of inaccuracy, it was widely agreed that Dickens's Mrs Gamp was a true portrait of the typical nurse of the day!

DETERMINED TO MAKE A DIFFERENCE

Upset by her parent's reaction Florence Nightingale wasn't about to give up that easily. She wanted to be a nurse, and she still wanted to be the *best* nurse she could be by the standards of the time. For two years, she would get up early every morning and secretly study medicine, to get as good an understanding of the whole procedure as she could. Part of her inspiration came from a woman called Elizabeth Fry.

ELIZABETH FRY

Elizabeth Fry, born Elizabeth Gurney in 1780 and married to Joseph Fry when she was 20, helped changed the British prison system. She visited many prisons and was horrified by what she found. Prisoners – men and women – were treated more like beasts than human beings. Prisons of the time were truly dreadful places. She campaigned for many changes, pleading that prisons be places for reform not revenge.

Elizabeth Fry argued that prisoners should be regularly fed and clothed and that they should have light in their cells. After years of tireless work, she got to speak to a committee at the House of Commons and even met the Prime Minister and Prince Albert. She made prison visits by women a regular event, and argued that cruel jailers had too much power. She died on 12 October 1845, but not before many of her caring reforms had been put in place.

Why couldn't Florence do the same good for hospitals?

A MEETING OF IMPORTANCE

Florence found it impossible to keep her passion for nursing to herself. Her parents were determined to get the 'silly idea' out of her head and sent her abroad. She went to stay with some friends in Rome and it was there that she met a rich Englishman called Sidney Herbert, and his wife Elizabeth. He was a philanthropist, which isn't someone who collects stamps – that's a philatelist. A philanthropist is someone who gives much of his money to help those worse off than himself. Sidney and Elizabeth Herbert strongly believed that all rich people should find ways to help the sick and the needy. Meeting such people made Florence all the more determined to be a nurse. Her parents' plan had well and truly backfired. On her return to England, Florence even went with Elizabeth Herbert to visit a hospital she and her husband had founded.

CHANCES OF BEING A NUN? NONE!

Her mind completely made up, Florence tried every trick in the book to train to become a nurse. She even wanted to stop being a Unitarian and to become a Roman Catholic – not because she now believed in Roman Catholicism, but because she knew that Catholic nuns were given hospital training! She offered to set up a special order of nuns, dedicated to the training of nurses ... but a Catholic cardinal named Manning saw through her plan and refused her entry into the Catholic Church.

DECLINING A PROPOSAL

Florence was living in a man's world and she knew it. It seemed so unfair to her that she couldn't – no, not couldn't but *wasn't allowed to* – do all the things men took for granted. In 1842, Florence had met a successful man called Richard Monckton Miles and he'd asked her to marry him. Now, seven years later, in 1849, she said 'no'. She said that she loved him, but that there was more to her life than being a dutiful wife. If she married Richard, she'd never have a chance to work and, to her, work was now more important than anything. Her parents were extremely upset, particularly because this 'work' she was talking about was dirty, filthy *nursing*! Richard Monckton Miles was upset too, but it didn't take him long to find another bride.

PACKED OFF AGAIN!

Once again, Florence found herself being sent abroad and, once again, her parents' plan seriously backfired. Florence learnt of a place in Germany called the Deaconesses'

Institute, at Kaiserwerth. There, the training of nurses was taken more seriously, and even people from 'good' German families worked there. The nurses were respected single women (often religious) or widows. This was where Florence wanted to go.

ON A MISSION FROM GOD

When Florence reached the age of 30, in 1850, she wrote that she was now the age that Jesus had been when he'd begun his mission of teaching. 'Now no more childish things . . . no more love, no more marriage. Now, Lord, let me only think of Thy will.' This was a big turning point for Florence because, up until then, she'd been trying to make her mother and father – and even Parthenope – understand why she was doing what she was doing. She'd been trying to get them on her side. Now she'd do whatever she had to, whether they liked it or not. 'I must expect no sympathy nor help from them,' she wrote. She would go it alone.

OFFICIAL TRAINING AT LAST

A year later, in 1851, Florence enrolled at the Deaconesses' Institute in Germany for three months (offering to work without pay). At long, long last she was really doing what she wanted and *needed* to do. In a letter home, Florence told her startled parents: 'I am as happy as the day is long.'

CHARITY BEGINS AT HOME

On her return to England, Fanny and William Nightingale had every reason to be grateful for their younger daughter's training and dedication to nursing. They were both ill, and Florence gave up a good part of two years of her life to care for them. She also became highly skilled at running the Nightingales' households. Despite this, she still managed to find time to visit hospitals in London, Scotland and France, and to write a monograph called *To the Artisans of England*!

THE ARTISANS OF ENGLAND

An 'artisan' is a skilled worker. A 'monograph' is a published paper or pamphlet. Florence Nightingale's monograph, addressed to the artisans of England, argued that human nature was really a force for good and that all the terrible things humans had done in the past allowed people to improve and do better in the future. She went on to argue that, whatever the Church might say, diseases such as cholera weren't punishments from God but the effect on 'certain states of [the] body, under certain circumstances.' Not bad reasoning for a thirty-two-year-old woman!

SUPERINTENDENT NIGHTINGALE

Florence had remained good friends with Elizabeth Herbert, wife of Sidney Herbert, the philanthropist (who was, by now, a minister in the cabinet of the government). Mrs Herbert was on a committee of a charity which ran a hospital in Harley Street, London. This was a private hospital for a very particular kind of patient. They were all sick governesses – well-respected women who had brought up children. She arranged for Florence to become the superintendent. Fanny Nightingale was absolutely horrified. William Nightingale came to Florence's defence. He arranged to pay her £500 a year to live on.

I'M IN CHARGE

Florence started work in August 1853, aged 33. Her work didn't really allow her to do any actual nursing; it was more to do with running the place. It was up to her to organize deliveries of supplies and to arrange service. She soon saved the charity lots of money. When she arrived, food was being delivered by the grocer three times a day, each time with a delivery charge. She had the food bought in bulk – much bigger amounts and less often, making real savings. She also had a dispensary for the medicines set up within the hospital, so that they did not have to send out for medicines every time.

THESE PATIENTS ARE TOO BORING!

Just fourteen months later, in October 1854, Florence quit. She'd been able to watch a few of the minor operations carried out at the private hospital, but she wanted to be more involved in nursing. She told the committee that the patients were *too boring*! She complained that they were either too ill with cancer to have any hope of survival, or were plain old hypochondriacs – people who moan about being sick when they are really perfectly fine! She wanted a wider variety of ailments, so that she could learn about different types of medical treatment and surgery.

THE HORRORS OF WAR

It was in that same year, 1854, that the Crimean War had broken out. The Crimea was a piece of land jutting out into the Black Sea and the Russians and the Turks were fighting over it. Both the British and the French sent soldiers to the Crimea to fight alongside the Turks against the Russians. There were many bloody battles and thousands were dying on all sides.

NEWS REACHES HOME

This was in the days before television and radio, so news took much longer to travel than it does today. People found out what was happening by reading newspapers. They published reports of the terrible numbers of dead, sick and wounded. The British paper *The Times* asked, 'Why do we have no sisters of mercy?' The French had far more – and better organized – nursing staff out there. It was now time for British nurses to be sent to the Crimea.

A CALL TO ACTION

A number of people's names were put forward to lead a group of nurses in the army hospitals but, as Secretary for War, Sidney Herbert thought the choice was simple. He wanted Florence Nightingale for the job. In his opinion, the most important skills needed were administration and discipline. Florence had proved her administrative skills when running her family's household and working as the superintendent at the ('boring') private hospital in Harley Street. It was also in Harley Street that she'd proved she could keep her staff in order. Herbert thought that Florence and her nurses would not only be able to help the poor soldiers but would, at the same time, convince the British that well-respected and properly trained female nurses would be good for any hospital, even back home in Britain. Florence was offered the job and accepted.

NOT A BANDAGE IN SIGHT

With the chance of a lifetime before her, Florence got together a group of the best nurses she could find. But it wasn't only nurses that were needed. She also arranged to take lots of medical supplies with her. These weren't paid for by the British Government, but with money sent in to a fund by readers of *The Times*. Government supplies were forever going astray. Shiploads of sheets and bandages were somehow ending up in a place called Varna, though the army had left there months ago. Some medicines were even ending up back in England! Florence Nightingale was going to make sure that her supplies came with her to her hospital.

TAKE YOUR PICK

Volunteer nurses were asked to come forward and many were interviewed, but most were highly unsuitable for the job. Most of the 'experienced' nurses were the very sort of untrained (and often drunken) nurses Florence was trying to avoid! The well-educated women from well-to-do families were equally unsuitable but for different reasons. Sober and well-meaning, they'd never done the most basic nursing task yet were offering to go off to a war zone! This left people who'd already done some nursing but were respectable . . . and there weren't too many of them about. Some of these were in Roman Catholic religious orders, so there was the problem of them taking orders from the Protestant Florence Nightingale. Finally – after a long, hard slog – only thirty-eight nurses were chosen.

SCUTARI, HERE WE COME!

On the 21 October 1854, Florence and her staff of hand-picked nurses climbed aboard a P&O steamship bound for the port of Constantinople (which is what we now call Istanbul). From there, she would travel to Scutari, the location of an army hospital in Turkey. But this was more than just a sea crossing. Florence Nightingale was about to steam into the pages of history.

THE CRIMEAN WAR

Florence was horrified by what she found at Barrack Hospital in Scutari. It was filthy dirty, there were rats everywhere and the patients were covered with body lice. The 'beds' were straw mattresses on the floor and there was hardly enough room to walk between them. Worse than that, the doctors were horrified too – horrified that Miss Nightingale had arrived with a group of nurses!

THE WAITING GAME

For some reason – perhaps they thought their authority was being threatened – the army doctors didn't want any of the nurses near the patients. After a while, they let Florence on the wards, but none of the others. But Florence didn't let the women sit around twiddling their thumbs. She put them to

work organizing the hospital stores and supplies, and sewing. It's said that, before Florence arrived, only seven shirts had been washed in the entire time the hospital had been there! Although she, like many others at the time, might not have been aware of the importance of hygiene to stop spreading germs, she certainly believed that clean clothes and clean wards would mean a better quality of life for her patients.

A BREATH OF FRESH AIR

When new waves of wounded soldiers started arriving from the Crimea, the doctors suddenly needed all the help they could get, and Florence's nurses were put to work. For the first four months that Florence had been at the hospital, she hadn't seen a single window opened on the wards. To say that the place must have been stuffy and smelly would be a bit like saying that an erupting volcano is a trifle warm. At last, Florence had the windows opened wide and the fresh air let in.

THE SECRET ENEMY

Germs spread diseases. You know that and I know that, but it wasn't common knowledge in Florence Nightingale's day. In London in 1849, for example, there was an epidemic of the disease cholera, but no one knew how it spread. The existence of germs was revealed to the world by a French scientist called Louis Pasteur in 1858 – four years *after* the start of the Crimean War. It wasn't until 1878 that he published his more detailed *Germ Theory of Disease*, so the information it contained couldn't have been known to Florence Nightingale, her nurses or the doctors. In the 1860s, Pasteur developed pasteurization – treating milk and other substances with heat to destroy any harmful microbes. Building on the work of the English physician Edward Jenner (1749–1823), Pasteur went on to develop vaccinations in the 1880s. (He was a very busy man!) Only then could patients be immunized against – made resistant to – certain diseases.

A LITTLE HUMAN DIGNITY

Many of the soldiers in the hospital had arms and legs so badly injured that they had to be cut off – though 'cut' may make it sound too easy. The bone would have to be sawn through. There were no operating theatres, so this had to be done on the ward . . . in front of all the other patients. This was horrible for the man about to lose a limb, and frightening for anyone who knew that it was their turn next. Florence arranged for screens to be put around the patient before surgery took place.

MUST HAVE FOOD!

Quite apart from their illness or injury, some patients didn't even have enough to eat. Florence's nurses would do what they could to get them food. Sometimes, this meant putting pressure on the nicer or meeker doctors to release more supplies! Much of the nurses' time was simply spent comforting dying soldiers in their last few hours . . . though no one seemed to know *why* they were dying.

DRUNK AND DISORDERLY ORDERLIES

Apart from Florence Nightingale herself, none of the nurses were allowed on the wards at night. They were dangerous places for women to be. Many of the orderlies – non-medical men who did fetching and carrying – were fit soldiers trying to get out of fighting, and many were drunk most of the time. Some of them were thieves too, stealing property from the dead or dying.

THE LADY WITH THE LAMP

At night, when Florence walked amongst the beds to bring comfort to her patients, she carried a lamp. This is how she got her nickname 'The Lady with the Lamp', which became an important symbol of her crusading work in hospitals. Florence Nightingale used the lamp so that she could see her way between the beds, but it came to be seen as a symbol of a 'guiding light', leading the way to better nursing.

SO MANY DEAD

At one stage, there were as many as 2,500 soldiers in the Barrack Hospital, with 75 soldiers dying a day. That's 525 soldiers a week. This meant that, if more sick and injured hadn't been coming in all the time, all the patients would have been dead in under five weeks, and the hospital empty! Florence made it one of her own tasks to write to the dead men's relatives, telling them that their husband or son had died.

NEW BROOM SWEEPS CLEAN

Apart from comforting the soldiers, one of the most important tasks Florence had set her nurses was to keep the hospital clean. She had them mop the floors as best they could, but these wooden floors were so rotten, there wasn't much they could do. All the human waste (yes, that includes poo) was collected beneath the building in a sewer, and the drains were blocked! Florence had the local Turks come in and clear them.

UNTANGLING RED TAPE

Official documents used to be tied together with red ribbon or tape, and 'red tape' came to mean the long-winded, obstructive official way of having to do things. Running the Barrack Hospital was full of red tape, but Florence did her very best to untangle it. If something needed to be done, she wanted it to be done there and then . . . *her* way. Some nurses later argued that Florence Nightingale created new red tape of her own!

'NO' TO NEW NURSES

When a new batch of nurses arrived from England, you might have expected Florence Nightingale to be pleased with all the help she could get. Far from it. Florence hadn't selected these woman and was less than happy with their calibre. She thought the well-to-do 'ladies' amongst the new nurses probably wanted to marry the army officers, while the 'working class' nurses probably planned to get drunk! They were certainly a mixed

bunch, but there turned out to be some genuinely dedicated nurses amongst them.

NOT JUST ANGELS

There was more to Florence's job than simply caring. Organization was all-important to her in all aspects of hospital life. She also used to attend some operations – usually the sawing off of arms and legs – and watched with great interest. Some nurses abandoned Florence and the Barrack Hospital at Scutari. They wanted to be nearer the fighting in the Crimea and to do more to help. They felt that, in some ways, Florence was holding them back. These included a woman called Bertha Turnball (who later, after a lifetime of nursing, visited the 68-year-old Florence Nightingale) and another called Mary Seacole.

MARY SEACOLE

In recent years, the work of Florence Nightingale has overshadowed that of Mary Seacole, but things are changing now. In her own time, Mary was famous, receiving recognition for her nursing from both Queen Victoria and Lord Palmerston but, for much of the 20th century, she was largely forgotten. Born in Jamaica in 1805, Mary's mother was a 'free' black woman – in other words, she wasn't a slave – and her father was a white Scotsman. Like Florence, she was a heroine nurse of the Crimean War. Unlike Florence, she went on to become a doctor. The story of her life was published in 1857.

THE SAW DOCTORS

Surgery was a very different affair then to how it is now. Today, we have anaesthetics and antiseptics. Anaesthetics help deaden the pain. Antiseptics help keep things nice and hygienic. The anaesthetic chloroform was first tested in 1847, but wasn't widely used in military hospitals. Antiseptics, on the other hand, weren't even developed until about nine years after the end of the Crimean War. Scottish doctor Joseph Lister experimented with antiseptic sprays and dressings in 1865. Without antiseptics or anaesthetics (which was a normal situation in Florence Nightingale's day) a simple operation could be a very painful – imagine having your leg sawn off without painkillers!! – and very deadly business. If the sawing didn't kill you, an infection soon could. In the 1840s, the record speed for sawing off a leg was about two and a half minutes!

BIGGER? BETTER?

Rather than having lots of new hospitals springing up nearer the fighting, Florence wanted her own Barrack Hospital to be made even bigger. Looking back on it now, this seems extraordinary! The hospital was crowded enough already, and more patients meant that disease spread to even more people. Where other hospitals were set up, most of them had officially appointed superintendents reporting back to Florence.

THE DISAPPEARING SOLDIERS

After a soldier left hospital, he was usually given time to 'convalesce' (relax and get better) back in England or in a special convalescent home before returning to fight at the front. What was odd about the sick and injured who were sent to Florence's Barrack Hospital in Scutari was that they seemed to disappear. A report in *The Times* newspaper said: 'It is strange that we have so few convalescents from Scutari. The hospitals there seem to swallow up the sick for ever.' The reason was, of course, that most of them were dying!

PALMERSTON STEPS IN

Lord Palmerston sent five special commissioners to Turkey and the Crimea to report back on the hospitals. Two of the commissioners were supply experts (they knew everything about getting the right amount of supplies – food, bandages, clothing, etc. – to and from places) and three were 'sanitary' commissioners who would look into cleaning up the army camps and hospitals. Palmerston ordered the commissioners not to interfere with medical treatment. He didn't want to upset the doctors and Florence Nightingale. He did, however, want them to improve supplies and sanitary conditions there and then. 'I am convinced this will save a great many lives,' he said.

OPERATION CLEAN-UP

The commissioners arrived at Scutari on 6 March 1855. They arranged the burial of dead animals, and had the yard drained and cleaned, and the sewers under the Barrack Hospital flushed out and the walls painted with disinfectant. They even added to the ventilation in the wards to let in still more fresh air. Rather than being angry at these men stepping in and 'interfering', as some expected she might be, Florence Nightingale was impressed by the

commissioners' work. She could see that these were genuine improvements and good for her patients.

BATTLE AGAINST BOOZE

It was the little things that made a big difference too. One of the things that Florence argued for was that the soldiers should be allowed to send some of their pay home. This would not only help their families back in Britain but would also cut down on theft and drunkenness. If a soldier had to carry his pay around with him, he'd be tempted to spend it on drink – or someone else might swipe it anyway!

Army officials not only thought that this was none of Miss Nightingale's business but also that it was a ridiculous idea. The government thought otherwise. Post offices were set up, and everyone was taken by surprise as to how much money soldiers did send back to Britain.

BOOKS, BUT NOT BIBLES!

Another thing that Florence wanted to introduce, at her own expense, was some basic education for her soldiers. She wanted books for the patients, but not Bibles. There were a few encyclopaedias in the hospital, and Florence saw how much pleasure the patients got from learning from them. She had many more sent over, along with paper, pens and ink.

A CHANGE OF PLAN

Not long after the commissioners left, the Commander-in-Chief in the Crimea, Lord Raglan, made an important announcement. Most of those soldiers who became sick or wounded in the Crimea would be treated in hospitals in the Crimea, rather than being sent all the way to Scutari in Turkey. Having been at the Barrack Hospital for six months, Florence was now relieved of some pressure and able to visit the Crimean hospitals for herself.

TO THE CRIMEA!

Florence arrived in the Crimea in May 1855. It was here that some of the rebellious nurses she'd clashed with had ended up working. It was also here that she clashed with the British Principal Medical Officer in the Crimea. This was an important title for an important man: Dr John Hall. He was not only, in a sense, Florence's boss; he was also the doctor who didn't allow his surgeons to give their patients anything to take away the pain when they were sawing their arms or legs off! He and Florence didn't get on.

TAKING SIDES

Florence wanted to introduce tighter controls on running all the hospitals in the region. She thought that they should all be run in the same way so that they'd work more efficiently. Dr Hall thought that it was none of her business and the rebellious – but often very caring – nurses, such as Elizabeth Davis, thought that things were going fine without Florence Nightingale and sided with the doctor. (Florence was trying to cut the amount of supplies some of them could have.)

In fact, Florence spent much of the last year of the war trying to establish that *she* was in charge. Much to the horror of rebel nurses and jealous doctors, this was finally confirmed in a general government order.

TAKEN ILL

Florence Nightingale herself became ill with what they called 'Crimean Fever' (high fever, skin rash, terrible headaches), which was probably a kind of typhus. She was taken to the general hospital in Balaclava (the town which the knitted hats are named after), and which she was in charge of. The Lady with the Lamp was now a patient in her own hospital! Here she was visited by Lord Raglan, the Commander-in-Chief. In a letter home, Florence described how Lord Raglan had asked her what her father thought about her being in the Crimea. She says she replied: 'He thinks his daughters should serve their country as well as his sons.'

Now see what it's like trying to sleep with this thing shining in your eyes!

MORE QUARRELLING

In October 1855, one of the hospitals near to the Barrack Hospital in Scutari closed down. It was staffed by a number of nurses from the 'unwanted' batch who'd arrived after Florence. To stress that they were still under her command, Florence accompanied them to their new posts in the Crimea, where everyone soon split into pro-Nightingale or pro-Dr Hall groups. There was a real struggle for power and the British Government sent a Colonel Lefroy to investigate. He took Florence's side.

FAMOUS FLORENCE

Florence wanted the public to know about these disagreements. She thought they were important enough to be debated in parliament back in England. The government – through her old friend Sidney Herbert – said that nothing would be gained by this. By now, Florence Nightingale was a heroine back home. News of her own illness had been met with concern. Her recovery had met with rejoicing. Her decision to stay, rather than to return to England, had been met with admiration and adoration. Surely it was better to make use of this positive publicity than to spoil it with in-fighting?

THE NIGHTINGALE FUND

In November 1855, Sidney Herbert seized upon the public's feeling of goodwill towards Florence by launching the 'Nightingale Fund' at a public meeting. The idea was to raise money to train proper nurses for Britain and to vastly improve conditions in hospitals. Letters of support were read out, including one from one of Florence's ex-patients –

who survived! – which described Florence walking amongst the beds, bringing them comfort, and included the line: 'We would kiss her shadow as it fell.'

THE MONEY POURS IN

The fund raised an enormous amount of public interest and staggering amounts of money. Queen Victoria sent Florence Nightingale a diamond brooch with a personal inscription, and an open invitation to come and visit her on her return to England. The famous poet Longfellow even wrote a poem about Florence, pinching the bit about 'kissing her shadow'.

PROUD NIGHTINGALES

After years of trying to put her younger daughter off being a nurse, and doing all she could to stop her, Florence's mum, Fanny, was finally proud of her! She did nothing to hide her delight, describing the public meeting which launched the Nightingale Fund as 'a glorious one'. Florence's father, who'd always been more supportive, tried to hide his wild enthusiasm with a more reserved 'Well done.' Sister Parthenope, who had acted in England on Florence's behalf on a number of occasions, was equally proud.

LESS POPULAR ABROAD

Florence was less popular amongst the other medical staff in the Crimea. In the spring of 1856, once her overall authority had been firmly established – and no one could say she didn't have a right to do pretty much whatever it was she wanted to do – she went to take charge of the Balaclava

General Hospital (where she'd been ill). A group of the rebel nurses, who had gone there to avoid working under her at Scutari in the first place, quit rather than be in the same building as her. They returned to England.

PEACE AT LAST!

The Crimean War ended on 30 March 1856 when the Treaty of Paris was signed in France. The Turks, British and French were victorious, having defeated the Russians. Florence Nightingale didn't return to England until the very last of the British soldiers had left.

THAT FIGURES

So how successful had Britain's attempt to improve the conditions in the hospitals been? In the five months of the first Crimean winter of the war, a staggering 10,000 British soldiers had died of sickness. In the five months of the second winter (after the visit from the sanitary commissioners) that figure had been reduced to 500, even though the size of the British army had doubled.

Some people later argued that this had more to do with it being a much milder winter than with any real improvements at the hospitals. Though the warmer weather probably did help, during that same 'mild winter', the death rate in the French army had more than doubled!

NO HERO'S WELCOME

The British public were clamouring to give Florence Nightingale a heroine's welcome on her return, but she had other ideas. She travelled across France incognito (in other words, without saying who she was) and didn't arrive back in England until 6 August 1856. Even then, she didn't go straight home to her family. Instead, she met up with some other nurses from the Crimea at the Convent of the Sisters of Mercy in Bermondsey. England was a changed place. Nurses would be taken seriously at long last.

MUCH MORE TO DO . . .

Since her return to England, Florence had received fan mail by the sack, and amongst the letters was one from Queen Victoria, reminding her of her invitation to meet. And meet they did, just six weeks after Florence's arrival back in Britain. Florence travelled to Balmoral, the queen's castle in Scotland, and met with Queen Victoria and her husband Prince Albert.

She soon discovered that while many people in the government wanted a very open and public enquiry into why so many soldiers had died in the army hospitals, the queen was more eager that it was sorted out very quickly and quietly . . . If the army could be proved to have made a mess of things, then the British public might get very angry!

THE ROYAL COMMISSION INVESTIGATES

Florence was pleased when the government finally got its way. There was a royal commission – an official investigation – into why so many soldiers died of sickness and disease. She had fought long and hard for this, and was delighted that at last the truth would come out. Being a woman, though, she wasn't actually allowed to be a member of the commission or even to give evidence at it!!! (Yes, I think that's worth three exclamation marks.) Instead, she wrote down all the facts and information she had and sent them to the commission.

THE HORRIBLE TRUTH

When the truth was finally established, it was not the truth that Florence had expected. She had always believed that so many of the soldiers fighting in the Crimea had died because of lack of food, hard work or no shelter from the harsh weather. She complained that many of the troops arrived at Scutari 'half dead' already, and died because they weren't sent there in time. She wasn't alone in thinking that. Most people thought the same.

Now the painstaking research of a man called Dr William Farr (who had the rather boring job title of Superintendent of the Statistical Department of the Registrar General's Office) showed that the biggest killer of all was the terrible lack of hygiene . . . and the worst British hospital in the Crimean War was Florence's very own at Scutari. Of course, she hadn't built the hospital and had done much to improve it, but she had seen it as *hers* and had been proud.

In fact, figures showed that *twice* as many patients died in Barrack Hospital as in any other British hospital! All the letters between Farr and Florence Nightingale about this subject were later burnt, apparently at Florence's request.

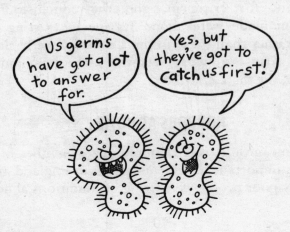

TAKING ACTION

It is impossible to imagine what must have gone through Florence's mind when she accepted this terrible truth. She had gone to Turkey to help save lives but thousands may have died needlessly in her care . . . Yet here she was being hailed as a national heroine! However awful Florence might have felt on learning the truth, she didn't try to sweep it under the carpet. She stressed to the royal commission (in writing, of course) just how important hygiene was to stop the spread of disease. She gave important friends and colleagues copies of a confidential report she wrote highlighting the mistakes at the Barrack Hospital. She wanted people to *learn* from these mistakes. She wanted to save future lives.

A BOTCHED-UP JOB

The British Government were keen to make sure that the royal commission didn't linger too long on the dreadful mistakes made by many over something as simple as hygiene. Neither Scutari nor Florence Nightingale was singled out for criticism, and the conclusions the commission made were about hygiene in existing army hospitals rather than those in the Crimea, cleverly shifting everyone's focus to (what was then) the here-and-now, rather than the there-and-then.

HORRORS AT HOME

Florence, meanwhile, was championing a number of new causes. It's important to remember that in England at that time, many poor people were living in conditions almost as bad as those in the early days at Scutari. In towns and cities many people lived in dreadful slums and half the children died before they were five. Thousands died of cholera and, in a country where windows were taxed right up until 1851, many houses were unbearably stuffy and horrid.

A BRIGHT IDEA

Window tax was introduced in England in 1695. The more windows your house had, the more you paid, which meant that the rich with their big houses paid most . . . But even a small house could have a number of windows, so many of these were bricked up to cut down on tax owed. Many old houses still have some of their windows blocked up. Now you know why.

I've got a view just like that at home!

THE GREAT STINK

The River Thames, running through London, was used like one big drain. Anything and everything people didn't want was poured or thrown into it – raw sewage (yes, poo again), dead animals and other things too horrible to mention. In 1858, there was so much *yeerch!* in the water that the river was too full of it to shift it all . . . The smell was so strong and so horrible that it became known as the Great Stink, and Florence Nightingale kicked up a great stink about it. The smell was so bad that people getting off trains at London Bridge station were throwing up everywhere!

TO BUILD OR NOT TO BUILD?

Another, rather different, cause that Florence threw herself behind was also concerned with London. This time it was to do with the location of hospitals. Florence thought that the best place for a hospital in London would be in the leafy suburbs, surrounded by parkland with plenty of space and fresh air. The doctors wanted the hospital in town, nearer their homes and rich private patients, so that they wouldn't have to travel too far to get to work!

A COMMON ENEMY

In both cases, Florence found herself fighting against the same man: John Simon. Simon was the City of London Corporation's Medical Officer. (The City of London is only a square mile in the heart of what we think of as the whole of London.) He was also the senior surgeon at St Thomas's Hospital and, when the old hospital building was knocked down, he wanted the new one built in the middle of London, not on the edges.

FIGHT FOR THE RIGHT SITE

Florence was backed by some of the resident staff at St Thomas's who agreed that she should design a hospital to be built on 40 acres of parkland in Lewisham. In return, she would provide nurses to train and work at the new hospital, paid for out of the Nightingale Fund. This never happened. John Simon used his influence to make sure that the new St Thomas's was built on the banks of the River Thames, opposite the Houses of Parliament. This was handy for him, and for his richer patients.

TOO MUCH TOO LATE

Another of Florence's arguments for locating the new hospital in Lewisham was that there were enough hospitals in central London already . . . and putting St Thomas's right by the river where the Great Stink of '58 had been, wasn't the brightest thing to do!

TIME TO ACT

The reason why Florence was so interested in St Thomas's, wherever it might end up, had a lot to do with her old friend Sidney Herbert. It was he who'd started the Nightingale Fund and raised so much money from the public, but Florence wasn't doing anything with it (although no one is sure why, exactly). Florence'd had enough of working in hospitals and tried to resign from her position with the Fund. Herbert wouldn't let her. You couldn't have a Nightingale Fund without Florence Nightingale on the board! In despair, Sidney Herbert finally arranged to use some of the fund's huge bank balance to set up a school for training nurses at King's College Hospital, London. Florence didn't want this, so suggested the St Thomas's Hospital training school instead.

TRAINED NURSES AT LAST

The Nightingale School for Nurses was set up at St Thomas's Hospital in London in 1860, and nurses are still trained there today. It was the world's first proper training school for nurses.

Florence herself never taught at the school, but laid down some very strict rules to make sure that the place was very

well-organized and ran smoothly. The day-to-day training was left to a Mrs Wardroper. Florence did visit the school on occasions, and there is a wonderful photograph of her (without her lamp) in later life, surrounded by a group of very respectable-looking student nurses.

NOTES ON NURSING

In 1859 – a year before the school opened – Florence had published a booklet called *Notes on Nursing* which, as the title suggests was made up of . . . er . . . notes on nursing. It was really the first manual for nurses and proved very popular. It was so popular, in fact, that it was republished in 1860 and again in 1861, this time with a special new section on midwifery (babies and childbirth). It sold millions and millions of copies all over the world and made her even more famous. At long last, it made her some *money* too!

ANOTHER 'NO' TO MARRIAGE

In 1858, Florence had turned down another proposal of marriage, this time to a man named Sir Harry Verney. Sir Harry then proposed to Parthenope instead and, unlike her little sister, she accepted. So Parthenope became Lady Verney, and Florence – despite her fame and independence – still had to survive on handouts from her father. William Nightingale paid for her food and lodging and gave her an allowance of £500 on top of this. It was only after *Notes on Nursing* sold so well that, for the first time, she really had money of her own.

SAY IT WITH PICTURES

Facts ands figures had become very important to Florence when she was trying to put forward her points of view. In the late 1850s she developed a way of showing these statistics as diagrams, charts and tables. She could, for example, clearly show the causes of death at different hospitals at different times using a kind of chart she invented called a 'polar-area' diagram. This hadn't been done before but was such a simple idea it soon caught on.

DEATH OF A MENTOR

On 2 August 1861 Sidney Herbert – the man who had done so much to encourage Florence in her work throughout her life – died, aged only 51. Florence claimed that he died of regret at not having reorganized the War Office – the government department which decided how British troops were trained, supplied and cared for in war! Elizabeth Herbert wanted to publish an article praising her husband for his lifetime dedication to the care of British soldiers. Florence wanted the focus to be on what still needed to be done to restructure the War Office.

ADVICE FOR THE AMERICANS

In the United States of America, things weren't so united in 1861. Civil war broke out between the northern states and the southern states, with the Confederates leaving the Union to set up as the Confederacy. The US Secretary of War wrote to Florence asking for her advice on caring for sick and wounded soldiers. She sent information to him and to Dorothea Dix who was the Superintendent of Nurses for Union Forces. Florence carried on giving advice right up until the end of the war in 1865. An American wrote that her influence and America's debt to her 'can never be known'.

AND SO TO BED

All this hard work, along with her earlier illness and experiences, had its effect on poor Florence. By the time Christmas came around, she was very ill . . . so ill that many of her friends and family thought that she might die. She went to bed and, for the six years that followed, it seems that she couldn't even walk. She had to be carried when she needed to get around. Some people claim that Florence was suffering from what we now call post-traumatic stress disorder – the horrors of war she'd been through had finally caught up with her. Others argue that she was suffering from a bacterial infection caused by drinking bad milk in the Crimea. Then there are those who think that she went to bed to hide from the world outside because of a terrible feeling of guilt about all her patients who died in that first year, in four miles of hospital beds.

I wish someone would **hurry up** and invent the telephone!

A BETTER PLACE

Being bedridden didn't stop Florence from working though. As her health improved, her bed became her office, and she got much done through letter writing. She was very keen that the sick and needy weren't all grouped together as one bunch and put in the same institutions. At the time, men, women and children were often put together in the same wards and the insane were put in with the sane. This could make hospitals frightening places, and Florence Nightingale wanted to create a proper system of care. She suggested nurses doing home visits, hospitals just for childbirth, institutions especially for the insane, and separate wards for men and women.

ON THE MOVE

In 1865, she (and her bed) moved to 35 South Street in London. Later, the address was changed to 10 South Street, but it was the same house and Florence never moved again. She spent the rest of her life there. It was from here, in 1867, that she gave her attention to studying deaths in childbirth and problems of illness in India. She collapsed again and after that she found it hard to concentrate as well as she had before.

THE JEWEL IN THE CROWN

In Florence's day, India was part of the British Empire. One of Queen Victoria's titles was Empress of All India, and the Indian subcontinent was described as being the jewel in her crown. Florence was not only interested in improving the health of the British soldiers stationed over there, but was also worried about the health of the Indians themselves. Having such a world-famous person as Florence Nightingale interested in the cause resulted in a health department being set up there.

OUTLIVING THE FAMILY

In January 1874, Florence's father William Nightingale died. Six years later, in February 1880, her mother died too. Parthenope developed crippling arthritis in 1883 and – surprise, surprise – Florence took charge of looking after her. Parthenope lived into her 70s, dying in 1890. Amazingly, Florence was to outlive them all by another twenty years!

LIVE AND ON CYLINDER

Even more amazingly, a recording of Florence Nightingale's voice still exists today. We're very lucky that she lived in the age of early photography, so we can look at black and white photos of her to see what she looked like, but very few people left a record of what they sounded like too. (This was in the days before CDs or tapes or even vinyl records, remember.) In 1890, Florence was visited at her house in South Street by representatives of the

Edison Company who recorded her speech onto a cylinder. Copies of the recording were issued in 1939.

TIME RUNS OUT

In 1896, Florence went to bed and, this time, stayed confined to her bedroom until her death. By 1902, she found it too difficult to read or write but still had a very active brain. She hired someone to act as a companion-cum-housekeeper-cum-secretary and continued to campaign for those causes she cared about.

HONOURS AT LAST

When Florence had returned from the Crimea, she had refused any honours that Queen Victoria or the British Government might have offered her. She had argued, earlier, that a monument should be built not to her but to commemorate the thousands of dead at Scutari. In 1907, however, the new king, Edward VII, gave Florence the Order of Merit. It was not only a very great honour, but the first time in history that it had been given to a woman.

A GRAND FINALE

Florence Nightingale died in her sleep on 13 August 1910. She was as famous then as she had been right after the Crimean War, perhaps even more so. Her death was big news and in all the newspapers, and the British public clamoured for a huge funeral. There were even suggestions that she should be buried in Westminster Abbey.

A SIMPLE SEND-OFF

In fact, things happened very differently. In her will she had said that she wanted a small funeral and to be buried in the churchyard in the village of East Wellon in Hampshire, near her family home. Her name doesn't appear on her tombstone – just the initials 'F.N' and the dates of her life.

ANGEL OR FRAUD?

For over a hundred years, Florence Nightingale has been treated as a saint by many, held up as an example of someone selflessly dedicating herself to helping others. More recently, some historians have argued that she was more interested in doing things her own way and being in charge than actually looking after people. The truth is probably somewhere in between. Florence Nightingale was only human, after all, but as the mythical 'Lady with the Lamp' she brought hope to thousands. It's what she came to *stand for* that was important. Modern nursing owes her a great deal.

WHERE IT ALL BEGAN

The house in the city of Florence where Florence Nightingale was born is still standing today. Called 'La Colombaia', it's a large white building on top of a hill on the city's south-western edge. A plaque on the outside wall talks of 'La Signora della Lampa' – the Lady with the Lamp – and her heroic dedication to the sick. Today, this fine and spacious house is an orphanage, where the orphans are cared for by nuns. Florence would probably have been very pleased with that.

TIMELINE

At home and abroad

1820	Florence Nightingale is born.
	Spanish Inquisition abolished . . . finally!
1839	Presented to Queen Victoria with Parthenope.
1844	Tells parents she wants to train at Salisbury Hospital.
1851	Enrolls at the Deaconesses' Institute at Kaiserwerth, Germany.
1853	Becomes superintendent at the Herberts' Harley Street hospital.
1854	Crimean War breaks out.
	Travels to Scutari, Turkey, with 38 nurses.
1885	Sanitary and supply commissioners visit Scutari.
	Florence tours Crimean hospitals.
	'Nightingale Fund' set up in England.
1856	Crimean War ends.
	Returns home 'incognito'.
	Visits Queen and Prince Albert at Balmoral.
	Royal commission set up to investigate soldiers' deaths in army hospitals.
1859	Publishes *Notes on Nursing*, reissued 1860 and 1861.
1860	The Nightingale School for Nurses set up at St Thomas's Hospital.
1861	Advises US government in American Civil War.
	Abraham Lincoln becomes president of the USA.
1863	*Roller-skates introduced to the USA.*
1890	Voice recorded onto cylinder.
1907	Awarded Order of Merit by king.
1910	Dies in her sleep.